# WHAT'S THE POINT?

## The History of Punctuation

Written by
Stephen Krensky

Illustrated by
Taylor Barron

A Sunshine Picture Book

CRABTREE
Publishing Company
www.crabtreebooks.com

Once upon a time there was no punctuation.
No periods. No commas. Not even a dash.

But that was okay.

Way back then, thousands and thousands of years in the past, there weren't any written words, either. Everyone was too busy just trying to stay alive. Nobody had time to write stuff down.

However, around 10,000 years ago, people began to realize that growing food would fill their stomachs faster than hunting for everything they ate. And eventually that gave them the free time to start thinking about other things.

Like words. Around 3500 B.C., the Sumerians in the Middle East created the first written language, a series of wedge-shaped marks.

This was a big deal.

And what about punctuation? Well, not so fast. The Sumerians didn't really need it to keep things straight. Neither did the ancient Egyptians, who soon developed their own system of picture symbols called hieroglyphs.

So when did punctuation get its chance? Well, around 200 B.C., the ancient Greeks started to write and perform plays. Plays had dialogue, lots of dialogue, creating a need for dramatic pauses.

But how would actors know when to pause and for how long? To help out, the Greek playwright Aristophanes introduced a series of three dots into his work. A middle dot meant a short pause, a low dot meant a medium pause, and a high dot meant a longer pause.

But outside of a few plays, the Greeks didn't care much about dots. Neither did the Romans who followed them. The philosopher Cicero believed that good writing itself would reveal where a text should start and stop. Of course, since he was a great orator, this was easy for him to say.

Meanwhile nearly all writing returned to what was impressively called scriptio continua. That meant there were no spaces, breaks, or other distinguishing marks between words.

Any further progress in punctuation stopped when the Roman Empire fell in 476 A.D. Assorted barbarians swept down through Italy from Eastern Europe. Pillaging and plundering were at the top of their to-do list.

Punctuation wasn't on their list at all.

Three hundred years passed before the outlook brightened again. Around 800 A.D. the Holy Roman Emperor Charlemagne decided that his people should learn to read and write. But what would help make that happen? Well, his scribes, under the leadership of Alcuin of York, knew where to start. If we put spaces between words, he said, they will get easier to read. (Until then, spaces had been left out to save room on the expensive animal parchments that the monks wrote on.)

But the monks didn't stop there. Pretty soon, they were also introducing lowercase letters, capitalizing letters at the beginning of sentences, and indenting the first line of a paragraph.

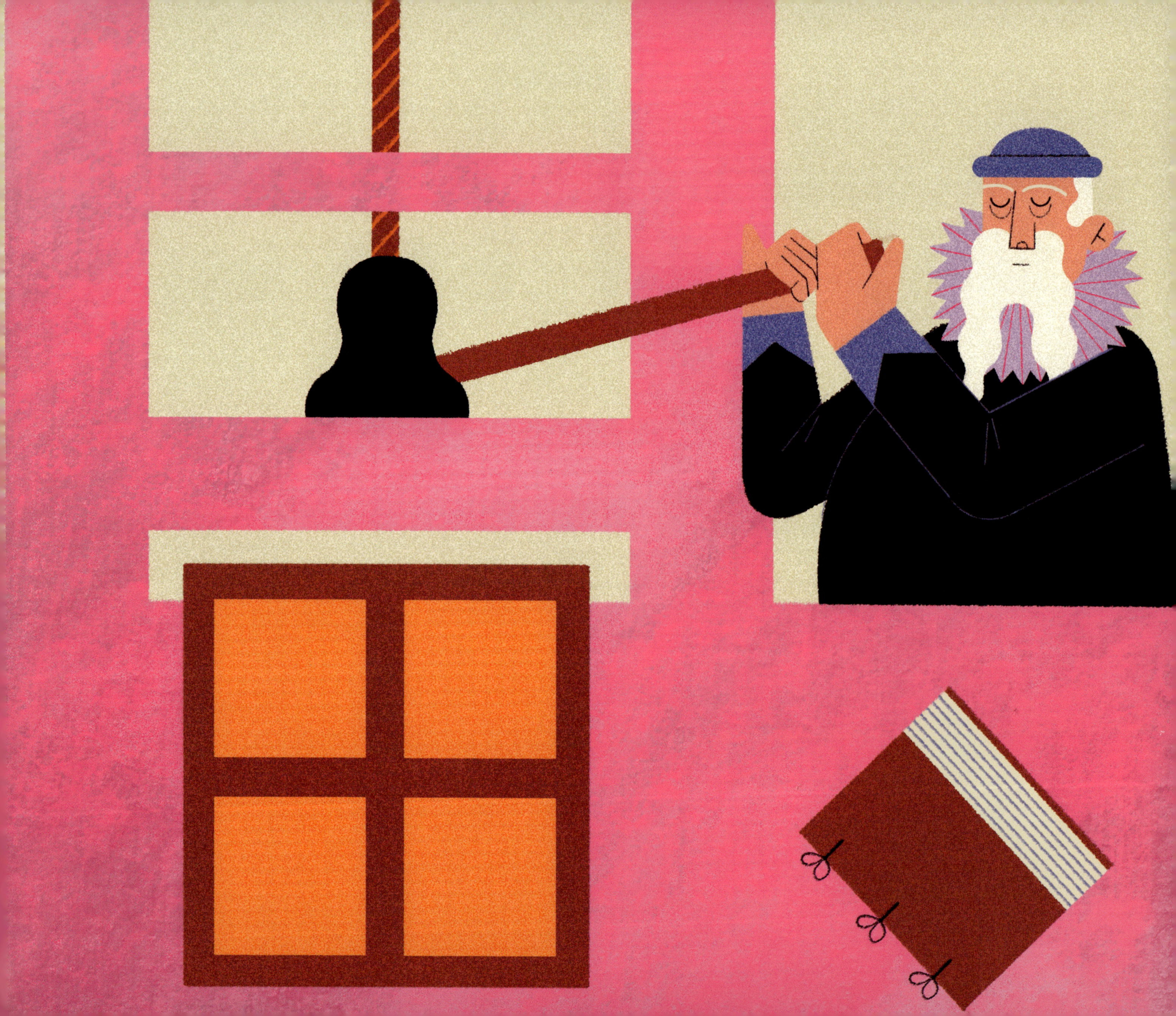

Things improved even more after Johannes Gutenberg converted a wine press into a printing press in 1456. When scribes had created books one at a time, they could pretty much punctuate as they pleased. But book printing concentrated publishing in the hands of a few printers near big cities. As a result, the rules of punctuation began to come together even though nobody was in charge.

Not surprisingly, the punctuation mark that got the earliest attention was the period. As the dot that ends every sentence, periods come in handy.

That, however, didn't instantly make everything clear. For example, William Caxton, the first printer of books in English, used the period both to mark the end of sentences and to indicate a brief pause.

Was that confusing? Absolutely. It took a little while for that brief pause to become a comma instead.

But periods and commas were hardly enough to do the whole job by themselves. How should questions be distinguished from other sentences? Why not add a question mark at the end? And when someone was excited about what they had to say, an exclamation point made that clear!

Apostrophes were added to show when one thing possessed another. Colons and semi-colons went to work breaking long sentences into smaller pieces. And two apostrophes put together became quotation marks—which surrounded dialogue to set it apart from ordinary text.

Not that everyone favored all these so-called improvements. A British nobleman, Lord Timothy Dexter (1747-1806) wrote a book called A Pickle for the Knowing Ones in 1802 with no punctuation at all.

When people complained that his writing was hard to read, Dexter published a second edition with a bunch of punctuation marks added to the end. If future readers were unhappy about the missing marks in the main text, they could "pepper and salt" with the extra marks as they pleased.

Although punctuation was always meant to accompany words, sometimes it managed just fine on its own. In 1862, the French writer Victor Hugo wanted to know how the sales of his latest book were doing. He wrote a note to his publisher with the single mark: ?

And his publisher, not to be outdone,
replied with a single mark as well: !

And even though letters and words far outnumbered the punctuation marks around them, sometimes the marks themselves required a lot of attention.

The Irish poet Oscar Wilde once explained: "All morning I worked on the proof of one of my poems, and took out a comma." He then added, "in the afternoon I put it back."

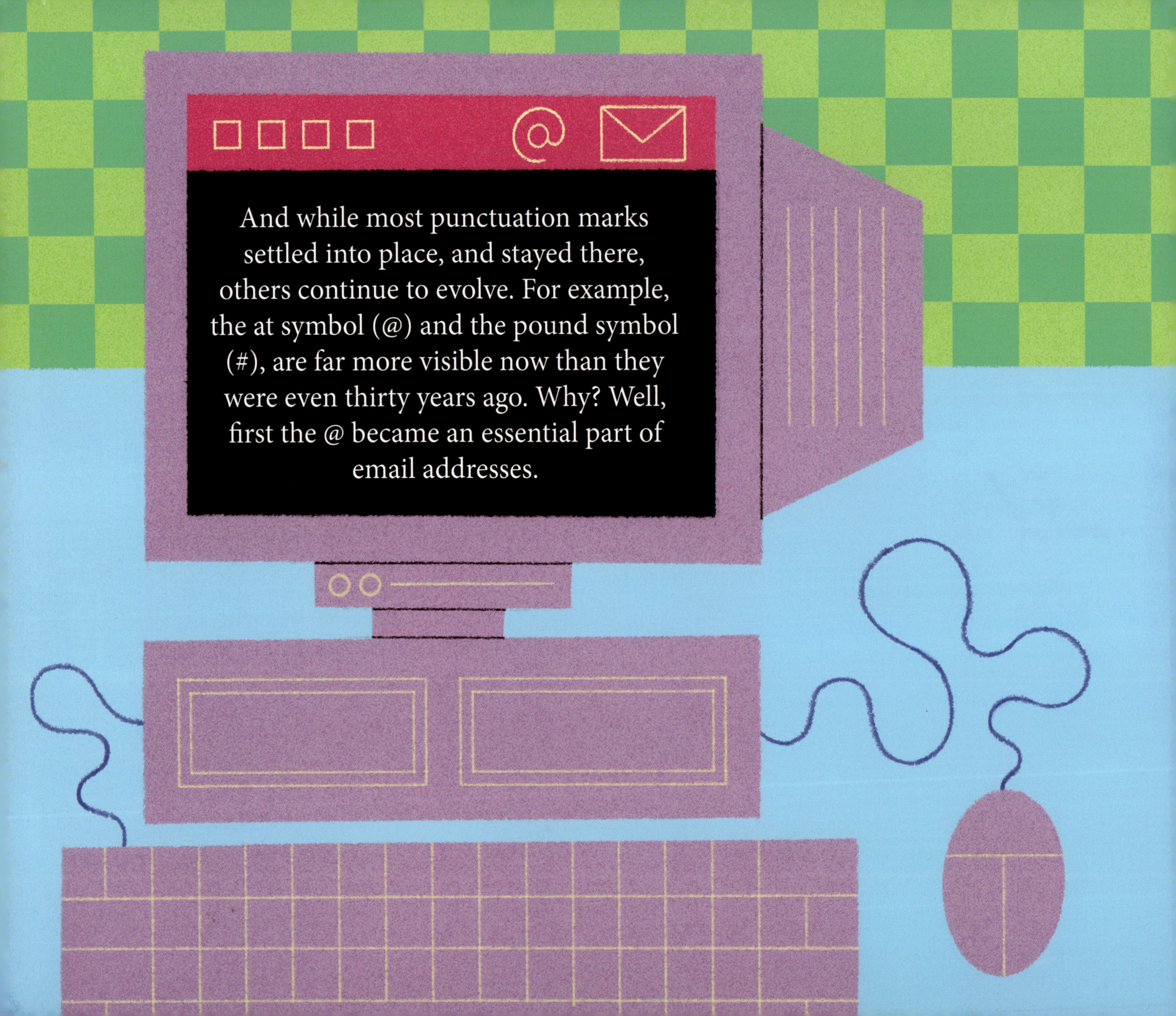

And while most punctuation marks settled into place, and stayed there, others continue to evolve. For example, the at symbol (@) and the pound symbol (#), are far more visible now than they were even thirty years ago. Why? Well, first the @ became an essential part of email addresses.

And then not to be outdone, the # expanded beyond its relationship with numbers to became an essential part of hashtags in social media.

So punctuation is in no danger of disappearing. As the writer Russell Baker explained, "When speaking aloud, you punctuate constantly — with body language. Your listener hears commas, dashes, question marks, exclamation points, quotation marks as you shout, whisper, pause, wave your arms, roll your eyes, wrinkle your brow. In writing, punctuation plays the role of body language."

Dotted or dashed, wriggly or straight, punctuation marks are now woven into our language. They may not have been here once upon a time, but they certainly will be here happily ever after.

# WHAT HAPPENED?

Look at the pictures below and talk about what happened in each one.

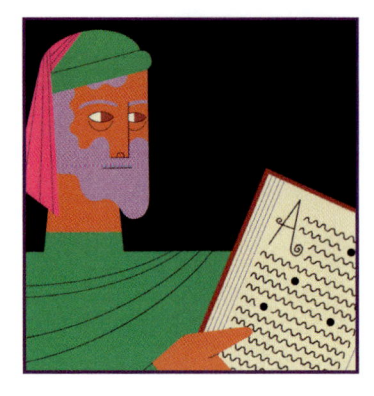

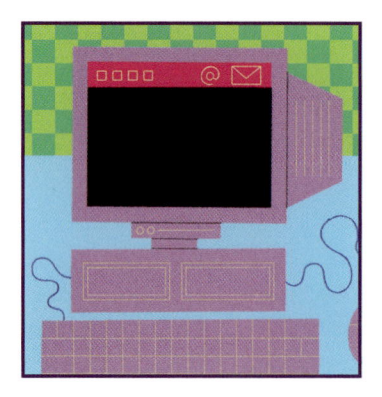

# WRITING PROMPTS

**1.** Write a sentence or paragraph using as many punctuation marks as possible.

**2.** List the different ways punctuation marks are used in our world today.

**3.** Make up a new punctuation mark and explain what it means.

## ABOUT THE AUTHOR

Stephen Krensky is the award-winning author of more than 150 fiction and nonfiction books for children. He and his wife Joan live in Lexington, Massachusetts, and he happily spends as much time as possible with his grown children and not-so-grown grandchildren.

## ABOUT THE ILLUSTRATOR

Taylor Barron is a freelance illustrator and concept artist from Seattle, Washington. She graduated with a Bachelor's of Fine Arts in Digital Art and Animation from DigiPen Institute of Technology in 2017. Her focus is in illustration, character design, and concept art. She loves playing with bright colors, both in her art and her wardrobe.

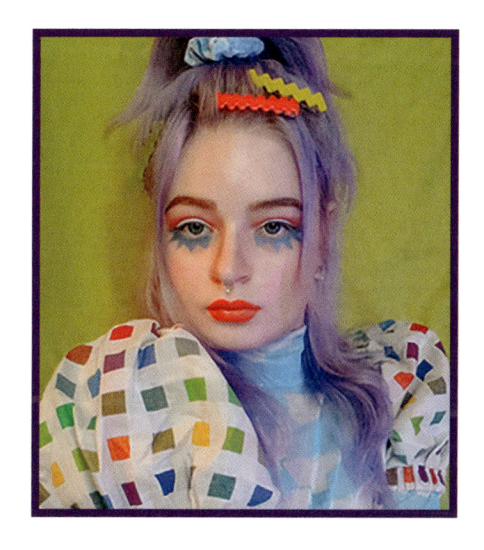

Harris County Public Library
Houston, Texas

**CRABTREE**
Publishing Company

Written by: Stephen Krensky
Illustrations by: Taylor Barron
Art direction and layout by: Rhea Wallace
Series Development: James Earley
Proofreader: Crystal Sikkens
Educational Consultant: Marie Lemke M.Ed.

# WHAT'S THE POINT?
## The History of Punctuation

Library and Archives Canada Cataloguing in Publication

CIP available at Library and Archives Canada

Library of Congress Cataloging-in-Publication Data

CIP available at Library of Congress

## Crabtree Publishing Company

www.crabtreebooks.com    1-800-387-7650

Printed in the U.S.A./072022/CG20220201

Copyright © 2023 **CRABTREE PUBLISHING COMPANY**

All rights reserved. No part of this publication may be reproduced, stored in a retrieval system or be transmitted in any form or by any means, electronic, mechanical, photocopying, recording, or otherwise, without the prior written permission of Crabtree Publishing Company.

**Published in the United States**
**Crabtree Publishing**
347 Fifth Avenue, Suite 1402-145
New York, NY, 10016

**Published in Canada**
**Crabtree Publishing**
616 Welland Ave.
St. Catharines, ON, L2M 5V6

**Sunshine Picture Books**

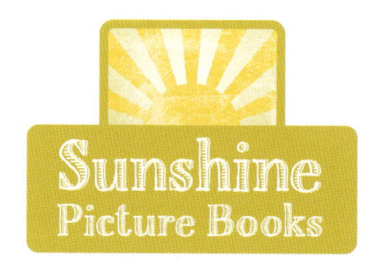